De(¢ent) Living

a  publication

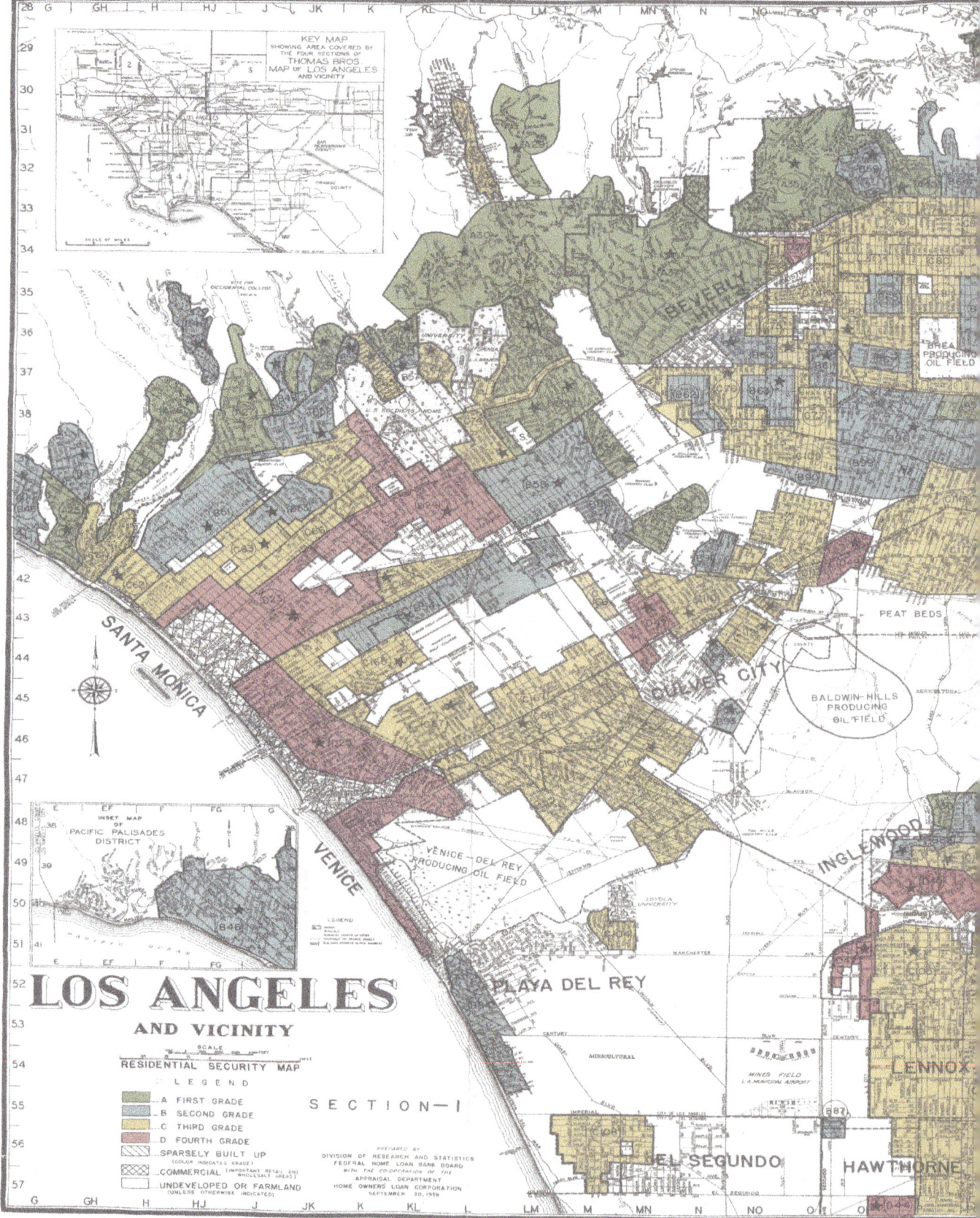

LOS ANGELES
AND VICINITY

SCALE

RESIDENTIAL SECURITY MAP

LEGEND

- A FIRST GRADE
- B SECOND GRADE
- C THIRD GRADE
- D FOURTH GRADE
- SPARSELY BUILT UP (COLOR INDICATES GRADE)
- COMMERCIAL (IMPORTANT RETAIL AND WHOLESALE AREAS)
- UNDEVELOPED OR FARMLAND (UNLESS OTHERWISE INDICATED)

PREPARED BY
DIVISION OF RESEARCH AND STATISTICS
FEDERAL HOME LOAN BANK BOARD
WITH THE CO-OPERATION OF THE
APPRAISAL DEPARTMENT
HOME OWNERS LOAN CORPORATION
SEPTEMBER 30, 1939

SECTION—1

KEY MAP
SHOWING AREA COVERED BY
THE FOUR SECTIONS OF
THOMAS BROS.
MAP OF LOS ANGELES
AND VICINITY

INSET MAP
OF
PACIFIC PALISADES
DISTRICT

SECTION 4 ATTACH

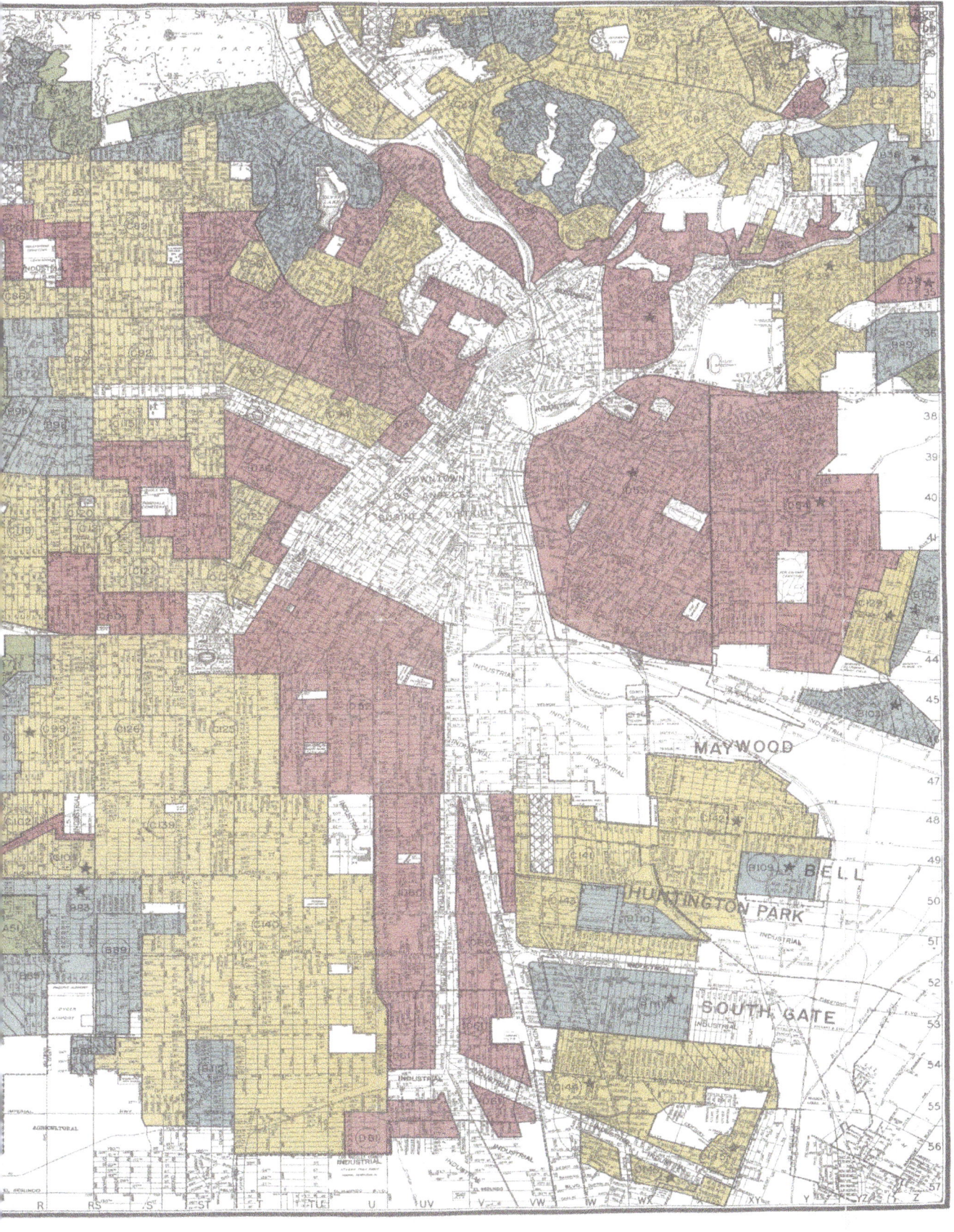

De(¢ent) Living

Cover Art and Design: Luis Antonio Pichardo

Publication Design: Luis Antonio Pichardo

ISBN: 978-1-946081-68-1

10 9 8 7 6 5 4 3 2 1

www.DSTLArts.org

Los Angeles, CA

Contents

Preface

Luis Antonio Pichardo

How does a person define a "decent living"?

That was a question I asked myself and my DSTL Arts team at the outset of this project. What is a "decent living" in our eyes: as artists; as nonprofit administrators; as members of communities that have been historically marginalized based on the race and ethnicity of our neighbors and ourselves?

I personally can't answer this question without reflecting on my own history.

I remember how difficult it was for my parents to buy their first home. I was about eight years old and in the third grade. Up to this point in my life, we had been renting a small, maybe 600 sq./ft., back house where I shared, with my brother, my parents, and the occasional relative from México, a single bedroom. The year my parents started looking into buying a home, my mom had finally landed a permanent, full-time job at the post office, the best-paying job she ever had. According to my parents, we were emerging out of poverty and into the "middle class".

My parents found their perfect home after finding a realtor willing to work with them. It was in the same neighborhood, only two blocks from where we lived, and it was as close as possible to my elementary school. Even better, it was within my parents's budget. However, upon seeing my parents's interest in the house, the white family selling this three-bedroom home openly refused to sell to my family because, as the realtor openly shared with my parents, they didn't want to sell to Mexicans.

In spite of our realtor's reminder to the white homeowners that the Fair Housing Act of 1968 made it illegal for them to refuse to sell to my parents, the white homeowners used an unpermitted garage conversion as justification for not lowering their asking price for the house, even though they had not kept up with any major home repairs. Subsequently, in order for the house to be insured and for a loan to be issued, my parents relented and paid, out of their pocket, for the necessary roof repairs and installation of gutters so that the house could become ours.

To this day, my younger brother has a scar on the bridge of his nose from where a section of a gutter fell on him while my parents installed the gutters themselves, as a cost-saving measure.

A few weeks after we moved into the house, my mom recounted this story of the home sale to me. She recounted this story to me because the two sons of the previous white homeowners had just broken into our new house and stolen a backpack's worth of mine and my brother's toys. She knew it was them because those same white kids were still attending my school, and I confided in my mom that those two boys let me know that they felt no remorse for breaking into our home a few days later when I saw them playing on the school's playground with one of my GI Joe action figures.

There was nothing I could do to get my toys back, and there was nothing to stop me from keeping a baseball bat next to me when my brother and I would be left home alone, especially after our house was broken into once again only a few months later.

Every person, every community, has a different definition of what a "decent living" should be. In general, though, it comes down to living with dignity: free of crime, free of social blight, free from persecution. There are specific human rights that most people see as essential for living "decently", such as access to potable water, quality food, and a shelter that is accommodating to the individual's basic needs.

There are many reasons why these things feel unattainable in this current age. Income inequality is creating a situation where more and more people are finding themselves working full-time jobs while teetering on being unhoused. Rising medical costs, inflation, and general debt are hampering people's ability to save for a rainy day. An advanced education is not only becoming more expensive, but it is now less likely to guarantee a living wage for most people. And then there's the legacy of Redlining, systemic racism, and vehicle-centric urban planning to contend with, especially in Los Ángeles.

A "decent living" is meant to be the result of a just and fair social contract, but in many ways, the principles of the American social contract have been eroded by a variety of governmental and corporate policies that go as far back as the Nixon administration. The social contract has not kept up with modern life.

I can't define a "decent living" for everyone, but what I can define is the nature of this book. This anthology is a collection of responses to the question, "What is a 'decent living'?" Poets, writers, and artists from across Los Ángeles have responded with their unique interpretations of the question, and without a doubt, most of us are advocating for a new social contract, one that treats all people with respect and dignity, one that ensures that we all have access to shelter, healthcare, quality food, clean water, and a living wage.

All of these things are attainable with consistent advocacy and collective action. The world does not have to be an unjust place.

If after reading this you find yourself wondering what the first step toward a new social contract might be, I encourage you to define for yourself what a "decent living" is, and then advocate for it with your local elected officials, not just for yourself, but for everyone in your community. It begins there. Together we can draw from our own experiences and ensure that all people are treated with compassion, dignity, and respect. It's important that all voices be represented through this advocacy.

After all, everyone deserves to feel like they have a safe place to call home. So, my neighbor, let's work on creating those homes for all.

Untitled 1

Angelica Castañeda

Making It

Carrie Traylor

I enjoy tapping into art and poetry, walking outside in nature, working as a caregiver, and connecting with family and faith!

Being constructive
or not. Moving
forward or halt.
Seeking answers
or questions. No
answers today.
Things in the
way. Unanswered
words. Nobody's
heard. Maybe a
bird. But that's
absurd. Life is
rotating. I'm
feeling lost. At
what cost? Can't
afford to live. What
must I give? I'd
love to have
no obligations.
Zero. Only

possibilities for
creation. Making
things. Making
things up. Making
things happen. Putting
life into action.
Not worrying
about making
ends meet. That's
a feat every
month. Pay
the rent. Pay
the debt. Pay
for the future, that
hasn't happened
yet. Breathe,
meditate, take on
a job. Step up, not
back. My faith
I'll pack. Wear good
socks. Hold onto
a rock. God with me,
my prayer.
Notes of peace in
the air.
Amen.

Postcards of My Community:
Rampant Gentrification
Series #2

Title: Prometheus Bringing Fire
Into Alvarado St.

Year: January 2023

Medium: Acrylic on canvas

Size: 22 ¾ x 54 3/8 inches

Prometheus Bringing Fire Into Alvarado Street, 2023

Dillan Garcia

I'm a multidisciplinary artist. My work investigates my mixed Chicano experience, indigenous roots, urban and green space designs, and gentrification in working class Latinx communities.

Pyramids Distancing In Between 6th Street, 2023

Dillan Garcia

The Home Owners' Loan Corporation (HOLC) maps continue to perpetuate systemic racism in low-income communities like my own Korea Town, and also Westlake, MacArthur Park, Pico-Union, and Rampart in Los Angeles. Attempts to revitalize Westlake/MacArthur Park have been few and shortcoming. Currently, a few housing projects have started development, and small changes in demographics are evident. These paintings document my personal experience with the park now. I hope my art brings awareness to L.A. City Councilmembers, investors, and developers about the negative effects of gentrification when communities are not considered or included in the decision-making process.

Postcards of My Community:
Rampant Gentrification
Series #2

Title: Pyramids Distancing In
Between 6th St.

Year: March 2023

Meduim: Acrylic on canvas

Size: 29 ½ x 53 7/8 inches

Redlining = Segregation

Dr. Rosie Ramos

Land of the Free… Mentirosos!

Streams of wild uncontrolled fires corral Latinos, Blacks, Indigenous people, and
      immigrant populations

Denying them the freedom to choose decent quality housing to raise their families

No conscience or compassion; you draw the infamous red-coded boundaries

      —to corral and control low-income and ethnically large populated
communities

      —confining the "undesirable neighborhoods" away from affluent
communities

Denying clean running hot/cold water

      —many families (including infants and seniors) shower with only cold
water daily

Denying updated proper utilities

      —many families use ONE extension cord throughout their homes

      —causing preventable major house fires and tragic family deaths

Denying nutrition/health food stores for minority families is an atrocity

      —not investing in ethnic low-income families is indecent and inhumane

Denying quality education from preschool through university levels

      —this means educating and hiring ethnic professionals that represent
their communities

      —this means providing quality free books and materials to properly teach our children

Denying quality healthcare—health insurance from pregnancy to the golden years
should be FREE

—learn from the COVID pandemic; so many deaths amongst minorities

Hidden hatred (in the minds and hearts) by affluent Whites has always plagued
people of color

—Ellos piensan closed-mindedly and cruelly that we are incapable
of coexisting

—yet selfishly they freely accept us to be their housemaid, babysitter,
gardener, and cook

I move where I want and breathe when I want; a blessing from God

Don't dare take away our Mother Land and Language once owned by our Ancestors
in the USA

You've corralled and encaged the ethnic minorities like animals into the most
depleted communities

—then YOU dare label our communities as less-desirable, hazardous
areas

Home Owners Loan Corporation (HOLC)

—DO NOT SEGREGATE ANY LONGER!!

Focus on what is strong

—productive, hard-working tax-paying low-income minority and
ethnic families

Fix what is wrong today; the Segregation-Redlining practice!!

I'm Here to Laugh Love Fuck and Drink Liquor

Jaime Scholnick

Jaime Scholnick is a multi-media artist living and working in Los Angeles, CA. Her work reflects on current social issues. She uses multi-media.

Detail: I'm Here to Laugh Love Fuck and Drink Liquor

Jaime Scholnick

The piece submitted is called "I'm Here to Laugh, Love, Fuck and Drink Liquor" (after the Coup song of the same name). This piece speaks about the hysteria whipped up when people escaping violence and persecution in various countries to the South of the USA came, en-masse, trying to cross the borders. Our Social Contract excludes people from other countries escaping persecution and poverty. Even though the USA is instrumental in creating the political and social climate in their countries. This piece was created in a one-week, manic state while listening to The Coup's song of the same name.

Crickets

Jeremy Forman

Jeremy Forman is a songwriter and librarian. You can go here to listen to the music: https://butterscotchstanley.bandcamp.com/

A Masters Degree
20 years work experience
Being a decent human being
Convictions
Making more money than I ever have
And still
Figuring out how few cans of tuna I can live on each week
So I can still pay the gas to get to work
When I come back
I pee and take notice of the tub
A cricket inside
I take my grandmother's mug and try to trap him to let him out
On my hands and knees
After 20 minutes I get him
But I notice one of his tentacles is off
Gone
The guilt sweeps over me
As I open the door and put what remains of him outside
Indifferent to it all, I receive an email that says,
"There's no easy way to put this: January bills are likely to be higher than usual."

And I worry that the little money I took out of an old Savings Plan last year is going
to cost me with my taxes because it's a "distribution."
I used the money to pay 10% of what it cost for me to move into this place

Roaches

Jeremy Forman

Couple the cost with the killings
And I see no legitimate reason to leave the house anymore
One neighbor drives a BMW
In another unit it's four to a studio
I get home and notice a piece of paper taped to my door
My rent is going up
Not the first time
In fact, I knew what it was before I took the paper off the door
That powerless feeling
I'd been here before
This happened up north too
And I fought with the city for a month
Until I just couldn't afford it anymore
And I found a place run by a maniac down the street
So, I took it
I started a new job the following week
And I woke up for work that first day
Monday morning, 5am
And there were 6 roaches crawling on the floor
Surrounding my bed
I scrambled for a sense of normalcy
Good luck

I went to the kitchen and put every glass and mug I owned atop each
        individual critter
I then sat in traffic for an hour and 20 years

Sawtelle House(s) with Two Workers in Driveway

Michael Shaw

Michael Shaw is an artist, activist, and podcaster whose work focuses on housing, housing inequality, and income inequality. He lives in Los Angeles.

24

Urban Landscape with Unoccupied Homes

Michael Shaw

My submissions are critiques of the cost of living, and the lack of a social contract, through the lens of housing. In the first artwork, workers labor on a house that they could never afford to live in; in the 2nd, urban housing is imagined as a group of unoccupied apartment buildings, homes which are only used for the purpose of investment, in the process creating greater housing scarcity and widening the income inequality divide.

Jack in the Box Drive Thru

Jesenia Chavez

Jesenia Chavez is a proud Chicanita, maestra, and poet who believes in the healing power of storytelling and community.

Been wondering about the drive-in at jack in the box drive-thru as I drive through a little buzzed hoping to sober up, I remember my niece works there long nights to pay off her car. She stays up all night and she gets promoted and her circadian rhythm shifts and she tells me about the unhoused lady she knows and her pets, and how she comes by once in a while and I wonder if my brother is a regular somewhere and someone helps him and sees him as a person and not just another addict in the streets with no family and I wonder if he gets to eat and I wonder if he gets to use the bathroom somewhere and I wonder why this jack in the box has become a homeless shelter and why so many people are on the streets and why nobody cares and why my brother is one of them now too.

now I am teaching

Jesenia Chavez

now I get a message, my brother almost burned down the house, now my sister is really pissed off and so is my older brother, and he wants my little brother to apologize, but he doesn't and he is off on the streets again, and it's raining so much, and I am out on the train, and I am on strike and I see so many on the train sleeping, and the cover of the LA Times says the train is dangerous and there have been fentanyl overdoses, but they don't say how expensive the city has become they don't say that homeless shelters are not permanent housing, and my coworkers are scared and a man is laying on the ground too close to the tracks and the security comes and they are trying to get him off and he yells, and everyone yells, and everyone is a zombie, a druggie, and I call for help and no one listens and they want papers and my brother doesn't have the papers and what if I see him? what will I do? and what will my coworkers say and I am embarrassed and I am ashamed and I am feeling guilty for being embarrassed and ashamed and when did this happen? and why? who do they belong to? who belongs to me? and don't we all belong to each other, me you, and my brother? and you don't care, and you can't care so you turn it off, but the crows are out tonight, and they are crying with me. And they don't leave their kin on the ground to die in the rain.

Untitled 4

Angelica Castañeda (previous page)

Otters

Joe Hernandez-Kolski

Joe Hernandez-Kolski is an Emmy award-winning host and two-time HBO Def Poet.
For over twenty years, he's run Downbeat 720, an open-mic for high school youth.
pochojoe.com

Who is this kid?
God, he's annoying.
I think he's the teenage child of some administrator here
Why is he here?
I'm here cuz I wanna stop feeling depressed but, hell, I don't wanna pay for therapy
          and my friend told me about this
"How to be a better you" class at LA Community College
And it's free?
Hell, sign me up!

But this kid
With his braces
And his oversized LA Rams t-shirt and his mullet
(Those are back in style?)
And his tiny little arms
(Do his parents even feed him?)
He's here giving our group his unsolicited advice
You know what I do? He says

I live by a saying
"I control my life
I control everything"
And although I don't actually control everything
I do control how it affects me
And then he leans back with this smug grin on his face

And the teacher says
Great... Thanks, Joe
Does anybody else have any thoughts?

And I say
Yeah, I'm sorry, I have a question

Joe, is it?
It's great how inspirational you're trying to be
Thank you
And yet

You've seen such a small sliver of what's out there
It's like you're looking at life through one of those underwater windows at the
       aquarium and you can only see what's right in front of you
And occasionally you see an otter swim by
And you're like "Oh my god, they're so cute. This is so awesome"
And they swim by a couple more times
And they look like they're having so much fun
But you can't see how big the tank really is
And you can't see the employees who are underpaid yet working another double shift
And you can't see the executives cutting corners feeding the otters expired fish tails
And you can't see the environmental groups trying to shut the whole thing down
And you can't see the otter
The otter pulls himself out of the water
And wipes the water maybe tears from his eyes

As he lies on his back looking up at the sky asking himself
Is this worth it?
I'm just doing tricks for tiny pieces of food
I wanna stand up for myself
But I don't have the words
Nor the skeletal structure
I'm literally built for flexibility
I don't control my life
I don't control anything

But
What about what I always wanted to do?
And so the otter tries
To tell its story
At late night open-mics
Deep in the valley
But instead it just picks up a smoking addiction
Out in the alley
As the otter's partner tries to be supportive but
"Why am I always the one putting the babies to sleep?
I come home from a long day of lab testing
And I've gotta put the pups on MY belly
You and I are supposed to hold hands not cuz it's sweet
But because I don't want to watch you float away"

And the otter floats further and further away
As kindergarten classes bang on the plexiglass!
"Do more for us!
Dance for us, Otter!"

And the otter dances and dances and dances

And sometimes when the otter is standing in line at the Best Buy

Just trying to exchange a wifi router that it bought last week but lost the receipt
Only to be talked down to by a teenager who looks just like you
The otter asks the skies… please just give me one break.

Cuz
Even if you can't see them, Joe

There are a lot of things that endanger otters

From pollution, habitat destruction, overfishing, poaching and a rising wage gap
that makes even two jobs not enough to survive in this tough aquarium water
Where ya can't thrive on tips alone

But the sea otter somehow survives
The sea otter refuses to just roll over and die
the sea otter has the densest fur of all mammals
even in the face of your egregious ignorant arrogance
The sea otter can and will withstand the worst weather imaginable

That's why you annoy me
Cuz you remind me of who the otter used to be and thinks he can be again

So maybe
Just maybe
Can you keep that in mind when you talk about how you live your non-aquatic life?

But that wasn't the question that I wanted to ask
What's the code for the bathroom again?

Untitled 2

Angelica Castañeda (previous page)

Otherwise Disguise

Alex Andy Phuong

Alex Andy Phuong (He/Him/His) became a published poet because Emma Stone inspired him to write passionately after watching her Oscar-winning performance in La La Land.

Facing life
And reality
Utilizing the poetic synecdoche
Of lending a hand
For the possibility
Of being grand,
And across the land
Far and wide
Near and far
People are
Who they are,
And then far away
Implies the future
Or a great distance,
But distance oneself
From negativity,
And instead hope
By coping
And understanding

The trials that all people face,
And then try
To do something wonderful,
And know that life could
Be amazing
With a better outlook,
And by looking around,
Become found

Dangle from an Angle

Alex Andy Phuong

Dangling from above
A height that is wuthering,
And even when fallen,
There is still the love
Associated with nurturing,
And while nature and nurture
Might appear as binary opposites,
There are still the plot twists
That make life like something
Dickens would have written,
And sometimes affection
Can make people feel smitten,
Yet understanding the care
That comes from the heart and soul
Really do alter perspectives
From varying angles,
Especially since being an angel
Or angelic
Is purely optional

Ancient Traveler

Katy Bishop

As I develop an artwork, I explore that the control we all want to exert in our lives is often paired with uncontrollable emotional responses. "Ancient Traveler" depicts one's struggle with personal doubt and fear as one searches to find housing one can afford.

41

what we pay attention to grows

linett luna tovar

linett (she/ella) is a writer, theater artist, and facilitator living in Pomona, CA, by way of Zacatecas, MX.

the little Children are parched in the valley heat.
they wither in cramped apartments, wishing there was a splash park down the street.
they're told, "sorry, but there is no money for that here."

the soccer Girls are starving after their game.
they had their last meal at noon and played till 5pm.
they're told, "sorry, but there is no money for snacks."

there's a group of Teens with boards who want to skate.
they go from place to place, and everywhere they're shooed away,
they're told, "sorry, but there's no money for your kind of play."

there's a Mother and her Children living in their car.
their clothes out of a trunk, their dinner out of cans.
they're told, "sorry, but there's no money to find you a house."

there's a twelve-year-old after school caring for her Siblings:
their Parents, at work; their playground, the street; their babysitter, a tv.

they're told, "sorry, but there's no money to feed your whole being."

there's a Child with a broken heart and an imagination itch,
nothing a stage, some music, and a paintbrush can't fix–
he's told, "sorry, there's no money for your creative relief."

and the Children, they go to sleep hearing the helicopters at night,
seeing through their windows the blue searchlights.
the Children, they watch the People With Nothing but a shopping cart
being arrested on the sidewalks.
the Children, who walk through metal detectors,
who don't get field trips but get fences and detention,
who learn the meaning of "deportation" before "graduation."
the Children, they see: it's true, there is no money,
there is no money for me,
there is only money to make me less free.

dear village, i am staring at a number string–
nine digits, two commas: 141545287.
a large sum of money that was always ours
to use as we saw fit.
i wonder, with just a sliver, 14154528, how
many splash parks can we build? how
many granola bars can we hand out? how
many skate parks can we erect?
how many homeless Kids can we house?
how many rec centers can we run with 14154528?
how many field trips can we pay for?
how many YA books can we buy?
how many storytimes can we hold?
how many instruments can we get?
how many puppets can we make?
how many concerts can we host?
how many therapy hours can we offer?

how many tutors can we hire?
how many Kids sent to college? how
many art studios can we open? how
many gardens can we plant? how
many murals can we paint? how
many athletes can we sponsor?
how many museum doors unlocked?
how many of these 14154528 monies
can we put where our mouth is
before the next photo op?
how many grassroots leaders can we raise?
how many queer Kids can we make feel safe?
how many free clinics can we subsidize?
how many talent shows can we host?
how much care, how much love
can we show
with 14154528?

and then and then–
how much bloodshed, spared?
how many young lives, saved?
how much crime, history?
how many handcuffs, obsolete?
how many guns, obsolete?
how many jails, obsolete?

*The City of Pomona had a General Fund of
$141,545,287 for the 2022-2023 fiscal year, with
51% of these monies dedicated to Pomona Police
alone and no line item dedicated to children and
youth specifically. The 2023 Pomona Kids First
initiative is a community-led proposal to allocate
10% of the City budget (in this case, $14,154,528),*

to services and infrastructure dedicated to Pomona children and transitional-aged youth.
"What we pay attention to grows" is a quote by author adrienne maree brown.

Untitled 3
Angelica Castañeda

Being In It

Mojdeh Amini

　　　　Being in Iowa
it doesn't feel like going
to any gardens:
Q gardens or
Rose gardens

Because we are in it
living with it
with our whole Being

Being in swing Iowa
Carduelis are Chirping
Corns are growing

　　　　Being in LA
it doesn't feel like going
to any theatres and watching any
Rich and Poor movies or
reading any books in such a gap

Because we are in it
living with it
with our whole Being

Being in beautiful LA
Crows are cawing
Citrus are growing

Being in NYC
it doesn't feel like watching any
horror   psycho movies
or reading any as such
horror   psycho stories

Because we are in it
living with it
with our whole Being

Being in live NYC
Alarms are screaming
Apples are growing

Being is Being
Iowa is still swinging
                growing
LA is still gaping
                growing
NYC is still screaming
                growing
Being is Being

in LA

Mojdeh Amini

How often do you get on the bus in LA?
Have you ever gotten on a bus in LA?

How often do you ride the metro in LA?
Have you ever ridden the metro in LA?

People
Buses
Metro
Lines
tickets
colors
clothes
classes
eyes
styles
ages
skins
smells
shoes
hairs

mobiles
naps
trolleys
wheelchairs
tears
laughters
smiles
weeds
smokes
can
papers
canes
trashes
noises
airs
waters
windows
clouds

Untitled 6

Angelica Castañeda (previous page)

Seeds of Transformation: Weaving a Tapestry of Social Justice

Rev. Dr. Dorthea E. Fondren

Rev. Dr. Dorthea E. Fondren: poet, author, and literary artist in Los Angeles exploring intersections of human experience, social identity, & nature through thought-provoking poetry.

In the tapestry of eco-justice, let us sow,
Seeds of change like flowers that bloom and grow.
Like a symphony, harmonizing hearts together,
We shall weather the storms and build a future that's better.

The housing crisis, a jagged mountain in our way,
Let's climb its peaks with compassion each day.
Like architects of hope, we'll construct sturdy homes,
Where people find refuge, no longer forced to roam.

The high cost of living, a relentless tidal wave,
Threatening to drown dreams that many crave.
But like alchemists, we'll transmute scarcity to plenty,
Creating an economy where fairness is plenty.

The social contract, a bridge that needs repair,
Let's rebuild it stronger with intentions laid bare.
Like gardeners tending to a diverse ecosystem,
Nurturing inclusivity with love as our anthem.

Empowering marginalized voices is our compass true,
Their stories paint portraits vibrant and new.
Like a mosaic made of different pieces combined,
We'll celebrate diversity and leave no one behind.

Restorative justice, a healing balm for souls bruised,
Rebuilding trust like phoenixes rising from ashes infused.
Like nurses tending wounds with gentle care and grace,
We'll mend communities and embrace forgiveness' embrace.

Let us be artists of justice, painting strokes bold,
Creating a masterpiece where compassion unfolds
With courage as our shield and empathy as our guide,
We'll shape a world where equality can't hide.
In this symphony of change, we'll rise above strife,
And build a society where all can live a meaningful life.

Untitled 5

Angelica Castañeda (next page)

Remain

a community-generated poem

They labeled no
"Low Income," "subversive
Racial elements." And proud.
Proud home owners
only the few.
Few opportunities due to few $$$
But not too few people.
Mi Raza.
It takes a village to raise
Familia— stand strong together!
Under one or
more roofs, we
thrive, strive, remain
alive.

They labeled us
"Low Income", "Subversive
Racial elements." And proud.

Proud home owners
only the few.
Few Opportunities due to few $$$$

But not too few people. [~~~~~]
  Mi Raza
It takes a Village to raise

♡ FAMiLiA♥ — Stand Strong Together!

Under One or
more roofs, we
thrive, survive, remain
alive.

61

Epilogue–On Redlining

Luis Antonio Pichardo

What is Redlining?

In the U.S., Redlining is an illegal, discriminatory practice where some services, typically financial services, are withheld or denied to residents of neighborhoods classified as "hazardous" to investment because of their racial or ethnic composition and/or for being primarily low-income.

The most common example of Redlining practices includes the denial of credit and insurance for real estate, but also extends to the creation of limited access to healthcare services and the development of food deserts.

Why Redlining?

In the 1930's, as part of Franklin D. Roosevelt's "New Deal" reforms, the federal government sponsored the creation of the Home Owners Loan Corporation (HOLC) to prevent foreclosures and the default of property loans impacted by the Great Depression. The HOLC was also intended to support the expansion of American homeownership by establishing credit-worthiness guidelines for future mortgage lenders and insurers.

Between 1935–1939, through the City Survey Program, the HOLC created color-coded Residential Security Maps of every major metropolitan area in the U.S. to indicate which neighborhoods would be best for investment. The maps classified each neighborhood by perceived level of desirability, implying that loans and mortgages to people in less-desirable, or hazardous areas, were unwise investments. These classifications were largely based on the racial and ethnic composition of those areas, in addition to the median income of those neighborhoods.

Affluent, predominantly-White neighborhoods were primarily classified as highly-desirable and colored-coded either Green (First Grade) or Blue (Second Grade). Residents of these areas could easily access loans and increase their investment opportunities.

Predominantly Minority- and/or Immigrant-populated areas, such as Black, Latino, Asian and Jewish neighborhoods, were deemed the least desirable areas for investment. These areas were color-coded either Yellow (Third Grade) or Red (Fourth Grade).

Residents of Yellow- and Red-coded neighborhoods were more likely to be offered either high-interest, high-payment, short-term loans; or they were entirely unable to secure loans for the purchase or repair of property. Such an inequitable policy purposely caused harm to these neighborhoods.

Redlining lead to deliberate disinvestment in urban neighborhoods; reinforced racial segregation between White and non-White communities; and contributed to the homeownership and wealth gaps that persist today.

Does Redlining still exist today?

Present demographic patterns in urban areas resemble the same historical outlining of the Redlining maps. In fact, U.S. Census data show that 60% of Los Angeles's African Americans live in neighborhoods where very few Whites are present.

Ironically, these same areas are undergoing gentrification: a process of neighborhood change that includes demographic and economic shifts in historically Redlined and/or disinvested neighborhoods. This is leading to the displacement of longtime residents, often long-term renters, which is having a profound impact on the social, physical and cultural wellbeing of the community's people.

While the Fair Housing Act of 1968 prohibits discrimination in the sale and rental of housing, it only added enforcement procedures 20 years later in the 1980s and did nothing to undo the segregation that the government spent the previous 35 years imposing.

What can we do about it?

We tolerate residential segregation because we're convinced that it happens informally—because of personal choices or subconscious prejudice. Perhaps we justify it as a desire to be among "familiar" community members. But what cements our separate neighborhoods is something most of us have forgotten—the government's unconstitutional and systematic insistence on segregated housing in the mid-20th century, establishing patterns that persist to this day.

To overturn these patterns requires various measures designed specifically to remedy the government's earlier imposition of segregation. For example, municipalities can repeal zoning laws that use criteria, such as density level and lot size, to prohibit apartments, and even modest single-family homes and townhouses, from being built in affluent, White neighborhoods. Rental subsidies need to be set on a sliding scale so low-income families can afford to live in middle-class communities.

There are many possible answers to this question. Contribute your potential solution to the impact of Redlining on our community in the form of advocacy. Share with our local political leaders your thoughts on compassionate, human-centric reforms that can create stronger communities and greater opportunities for living a "decent life". Let them know how you envision our new Social Contract.

To find your political representative and begin the work of advocating for dignified living standards, a new Social Contract, visit the following websites.

If you live in the City of Los Angeles, use this tool to find your representatives:

- http://neighborhoodinfo.lacity.org

If you live in the County of Los Angeles, use this tool to find your representatives:

- http://rrcc.lacounty.gov/OnlineDistrictmapApp

To find your State of California representatives only, use this tool:

- http://findyourrep.legislature.ca.gov

To find your federal representatives only, use these tools:

- https://www.house.gov/representatives/find-your-representative

- https://www.senate.gov/senators/senators-contact.htm

Search a directory of the HOLCs Redlining maps thanks to the efforts of the University of Richmond's *Mapping Inequality* project at:

- https://dsl.richmond.edu/panorama/redlining/
  (the HOLC map of Los Angeles is on the following pages)

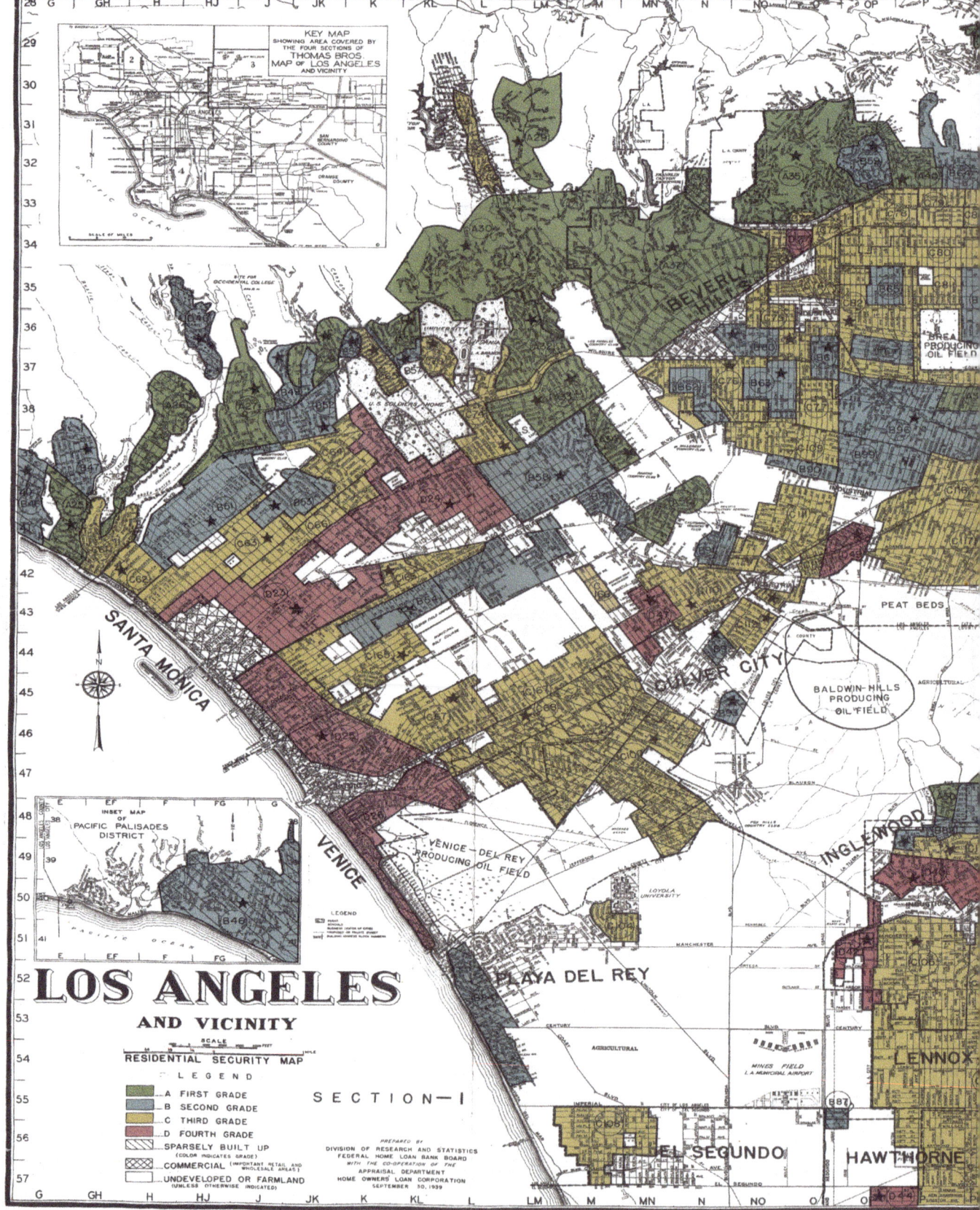

LOS ANGELES
AND VICINITY

SCALE

RESIDENTIAL SECURITY MAP

LEGEND

- A FIRST GRADE
- B SECOND GRADE
- C THIRD GRADE
- D FOURTH GRADE
- SPARSELY BUILT UP
  (COLOR INDICATES GRADE)
- COMMERCIAL (IMPORTANT RETAIL AND WHOLESALE AREAS)
- UNDEVELOPED OR FARMLAND
  (UNLESS OTHERWISE INDICATED)

SECTION-1

PREPARED BY
DIVISION OF RESEARCH AND STATISTICS
FEDERAL HOME LOAN BANK BOARD
WITH THE CO-OPERATION OF THE
APPRAISAL DEPARTMENT
HOME OWNERS' LOAN CORPORATION
SEPTEMBER 30, 1939

KEY MAP
SHOWING AREA COVERED BY
THE FOUR SECTIONS OF
THOMAS BROS.
MAP OF LOS ANGELES
AND VICINITY

INSET MAP
OF
PACIFIC PALISADES
DISTRICT

SECTION 4 ATTACH

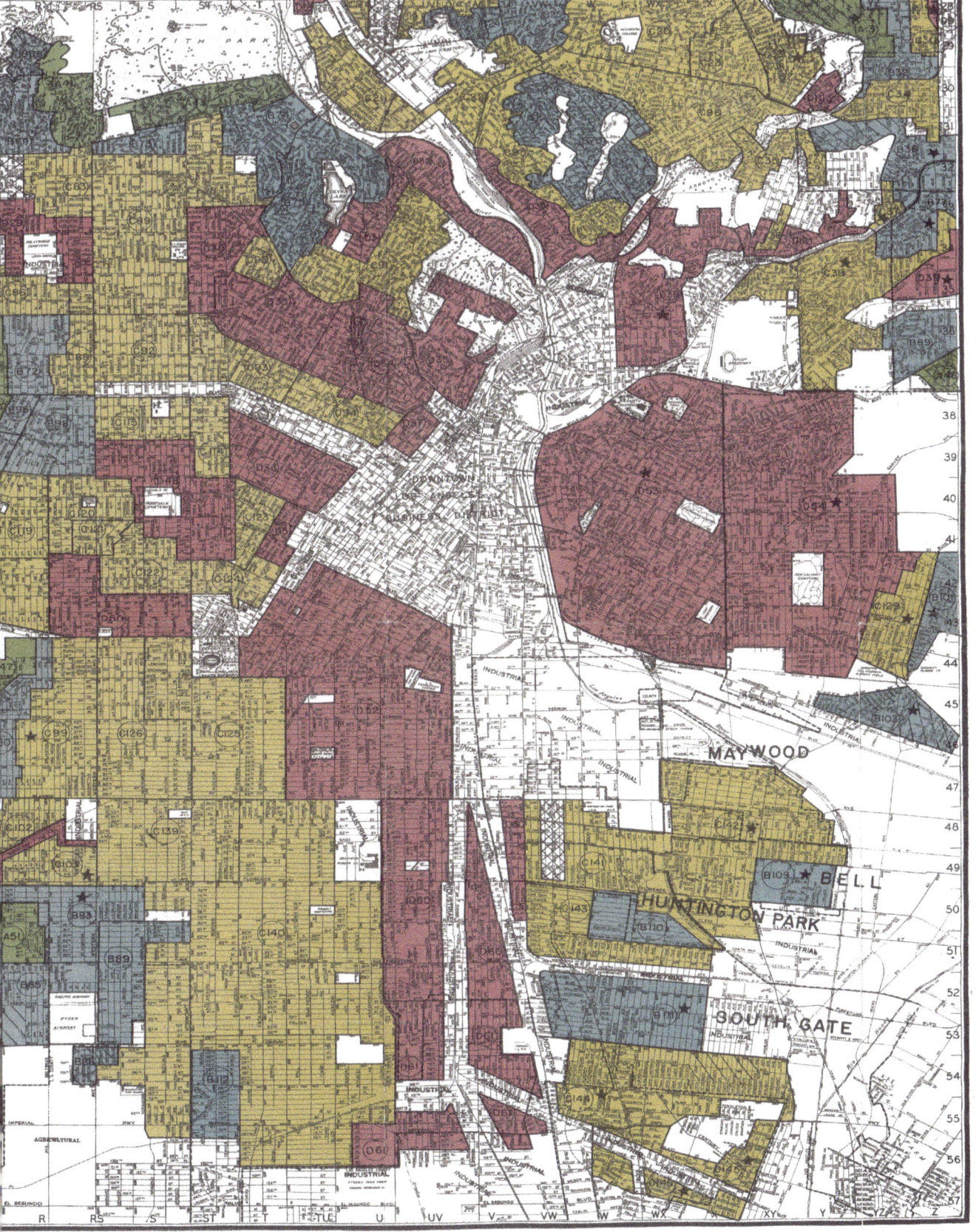

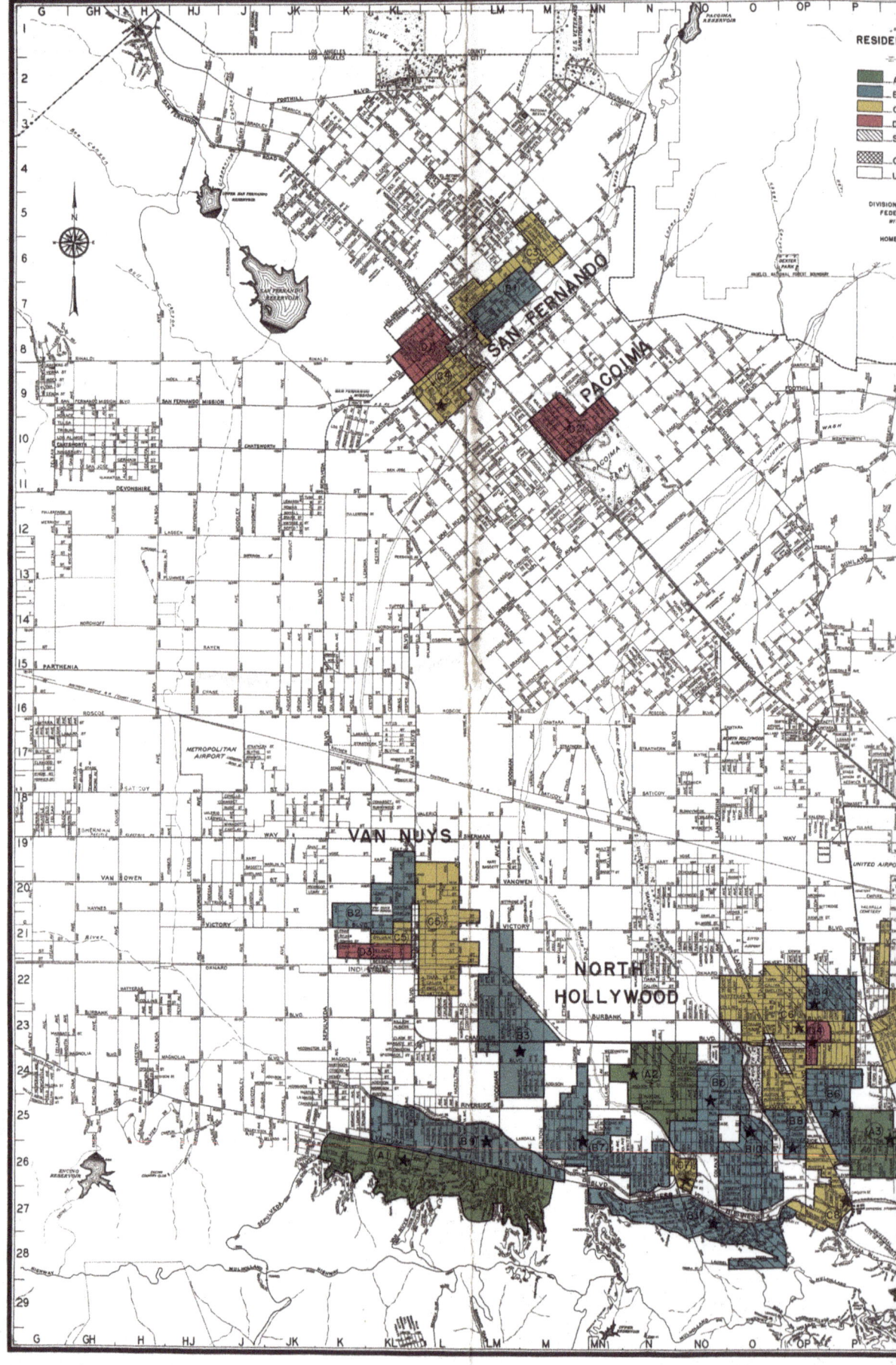

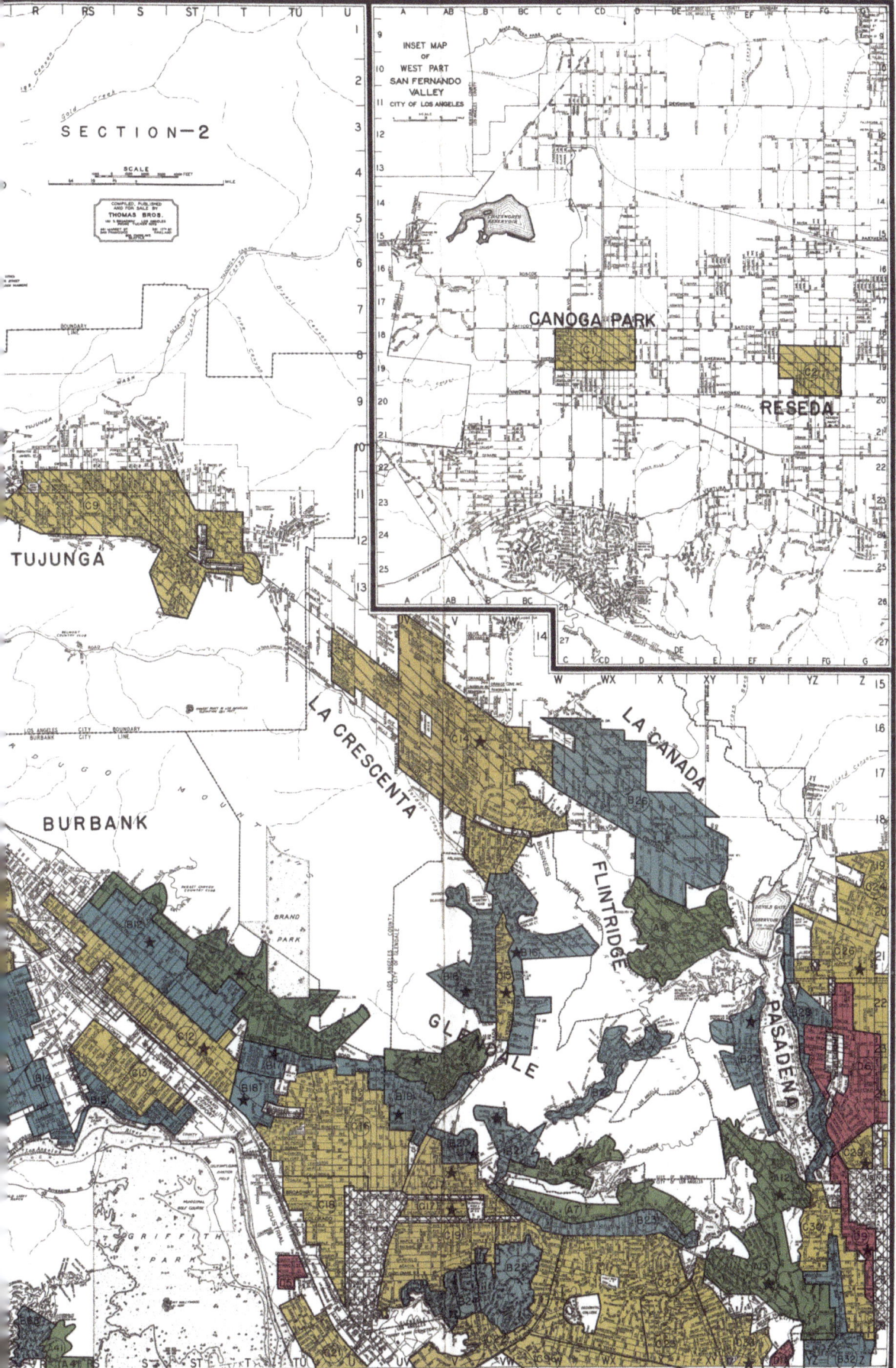

SECTION—2

SCALE

COMPILED, PUBLISHED
AND FOR SALE BY
THOMAS BROS.

INSET MAP
OF
WEST PART
SAN FERNANDO
VALLEY
CITY OF LOS ANGELES

CANOGA PARK

RESEDA

TUJUNGA

BURBANK

LA CRESCENTA

LA CAÑADA

FLINTRIDGE

GLENDALE

PASADENA

GRIFFITH PARK

THOMAS BROS.
Map of
PASADENA,
ALHAMBRA, POMONA,
SOUTH PASADENA, ONTARIO,
MONROVIA, SAN GABRIEL, ARCADIA,
AZUSA, UPLAND, SAN MARINO, ALTADENA,
SIERRA MADRE,   EL MONTE,   LA VERNE,
COVINA, GLENDORA, CLAREMONT, ROSEMEAD,
SAN DIMAS, BALDWIN PARK, DUARTE, TEMPLE CITY,
WILMAR, WEST COVINA,   AND VICINITY

SCALE

COMPILED, PUBLISHED
AND FOR SALE BY
THOMAS BROS.

© BY GEO. C. THOMAS

SECTION — 3

KEY MAP
SHOWING AREA
COVERED BY THIS MAP

RESIDENTIAL SECURITY MAP

— L E G E N D —

A FIRST GRADE
B SECOND GRADE
C THIRD GRADE
D FOURTH GRADE
SPARSELY BUILT UP
(COLOR INDICATES GRADE)
COMMERCIAL (IMPORTANT RETAIL AND WHOLESALE AREAS)
UNDEVELOPED OR FARMLAND
(UNLESS OTHERWISE INDICATED)

PREPARED BY
DIVISION OF RESEARCH AND STATISTICS
FEDERAL HOME LOAN BANK BOARD
WITH THE CO-OPERATION OF THE
APPRAISAL DEPARTMENT
HOME OWNERS LOAN CORPORATION
SEPTEMBER 30, 1939

LEGEND

ALTADENA

SIERRA MADRE

ARCADIA

SAN MARINO

ALHAMBRA

SAN GABRIEL

TEMPLE CITY

ROSEMEAD

MONTEREY PARK

PASADENA SEWER FARM

WESTERN AIR EXPRESS

SECTION 2 ATTACHES HERE

SECTION 1 ATTACHES HERE

SECTION 4 ATTACHES HERE

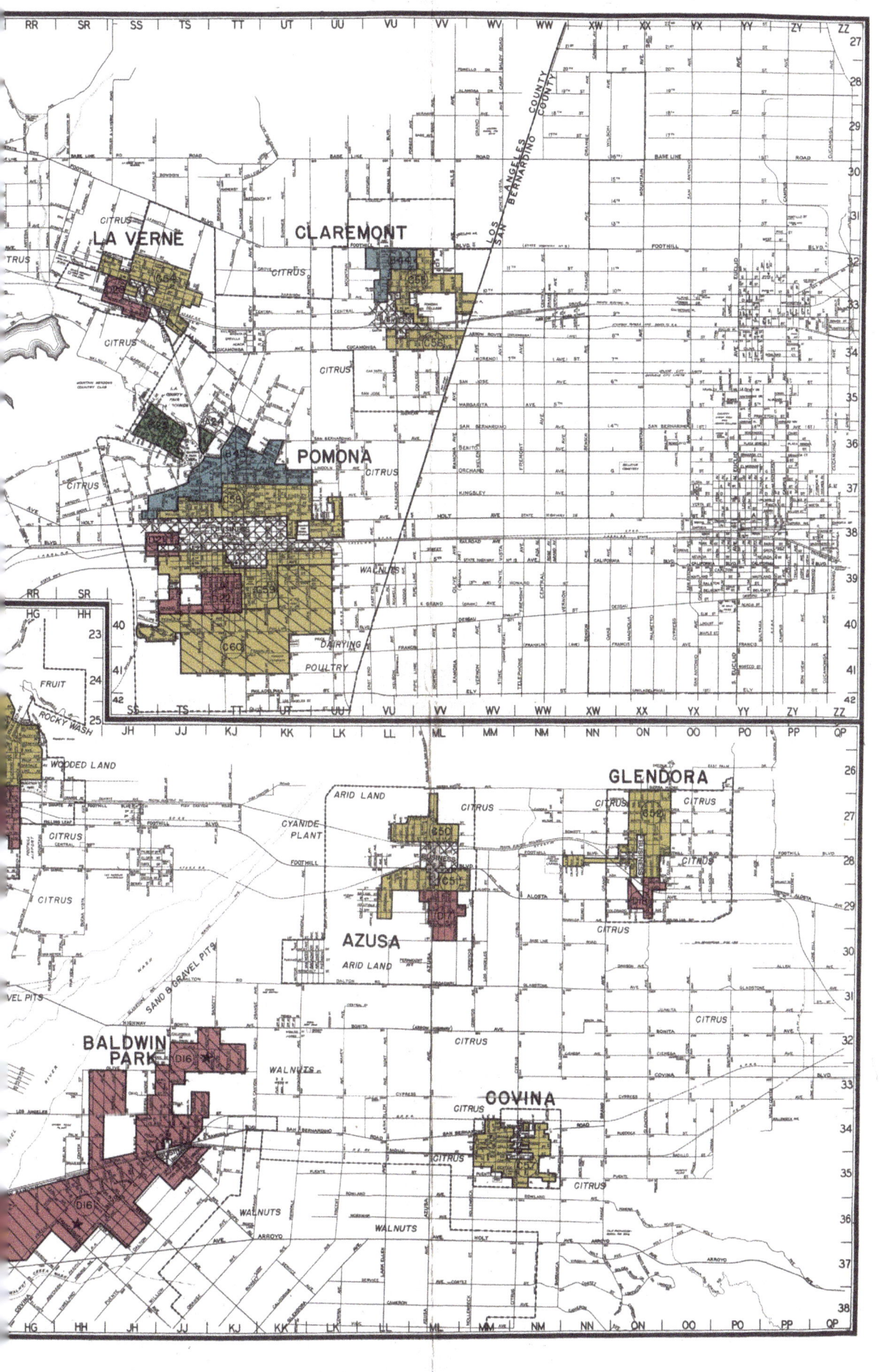

SECTION 3 ATTACHES HERE

SECTION I ATTACHES HERE

MONTEREY PARK

MONTEBELLO

PICO

WHITTIER

RIVERA

DOWNEY

CLEARWATER

BELLFLOWER

NORWALK

AGRICULTURAL

HYNES

ARTESIA

AGRICULTURAL

LOS ANGELES CO.
ORANGE CO.

THOMAS BROS.
Map of
WHITTIER
MONTEBELLO
BELVEDERE
ARTESIA, BELLFLOWER, CLEARWATER,
DOWNEY, HYNES, NORWALK, RIVERA,
PICO, SANTA FE SPRINGS & VICINITY
SCALE

KEY MAP
SHOWING AREA COVERED BY
THE FOUR SECTIONS OF
THOMAS BROS.
MAP of LOS ANGELES
AND VICINITY

SAN FERNANDO

MT. LOWE

2

3

PASADENA

LOS ANGELES

BEVERLY HILLS

SANTA MONICA

1

SAN
BERNARDINO
COUNTY

PACIFIC OCEAN

REDONDO BEACH

4

ORANGE
COUNTY

N

SAN PEDRO

SCALE OF MILES

COMPILED, PUBLISHED
AND FOR SALE BY
THOMAS BROS.

MANHATTAN BEACH

HERMOSA BEACH

REDONDO BEACH

EL SEGUNDO TANK FARM
STANDARD OIL CO.

COMPTON

CENTER

57

58

59

60

61

62

63

64

65

66

67

68

69

70

71

72

73

74

75

76

77

78

79

80

81

82

83

84

85

REDONDO-TORRANCE

SEPULVEDA

N

PALOS VERDES

PALOS VERDES
GOLF COURSE

AGRICULTURAL

AGRICULTURAL

SECTION — 4

RESIDENTIAL

LEGEND

A FIR...
B SE...
C TH...
D FO...
SPAR...
(COL...)
COMM...
UNDE...

SCALE

DIVISION OF
FEDERAL
WITH THE
APPR...
HOME OWN...
SE...

LM M MN N NO O OP P

INSET MAP
OF
SOUTHEAST PART OF
LONG BEACH

About the DSTL Arts Creative Impact Workshops and Books

Elevating voices to empower our community—that is the goal of our Creative Impact artist-led workshops and anthologies.

Teaching Artist Interns from our Poet/Artist Development Program collaborate with DSTL Arts staff to develop workshop topics related to social justice, community development, and the overall well-being of our local communities, and offer instruction in tools for creative expression that can be used to address those same issues.

Annually, these workshops culminate in the release and public reading of a community-generated anthology of poetry, art, and more, further celebrating the unique voices of our diverse community members.

For more information, locations, and dates for upcoming Creative Impact Workshops, contact us by email at info@DSTLArts.org today.

This program is supported in part by:

Sobre los Talleres y Libros Impacto Creativo de DSTL Arts

Elevando voces para empoderar nuestra comunidad—ese es el propósito de nuestros talleres presentados por artistas y las antologías de Impacto Creativo.

Maestros Aprendices de Arte de nuestro Programa para el Desarrollo de Poeta/Artistas colaboran con el personal de DSTL Arts para desarrollar temas para talleres relacionados a la justicia social, la urbanización comunitaria, y el bienestar en general de nuestras comunidades locales, y ofrecen instrucción sobre herramientas para la expresión creativa cuales se pueden usar para abordar esas mismas temas.

Cada año, estos talleres culminan con la publicación y presentación pública de una antología comunitaria de poesía, arte, y más, aumentando la celebración de las voces únicas de nuestros miembros diversos de la comunidad.

Para más información, localidades, y fechas de los próximos talleres de Impacto Creativo, comuníquense por correo electrónico al info@DSTLArts.org.

Este programa recibe apoyo en parte por:

Previous Creative Impact Anthologies

community bridges

A Reflection on Civil Rights

a DSTL arts publication

Community Bridges: A Reflection on Civil Rights
an examination of the impact of the Civil Rights Movement on modern day society
Available now at DSTLArts.org/shop

Previous Creative Impact Anthologies

Héroes de Los Angeles
celebrating the personal heroes of our community members
Available now at DSTLArts.org/shop

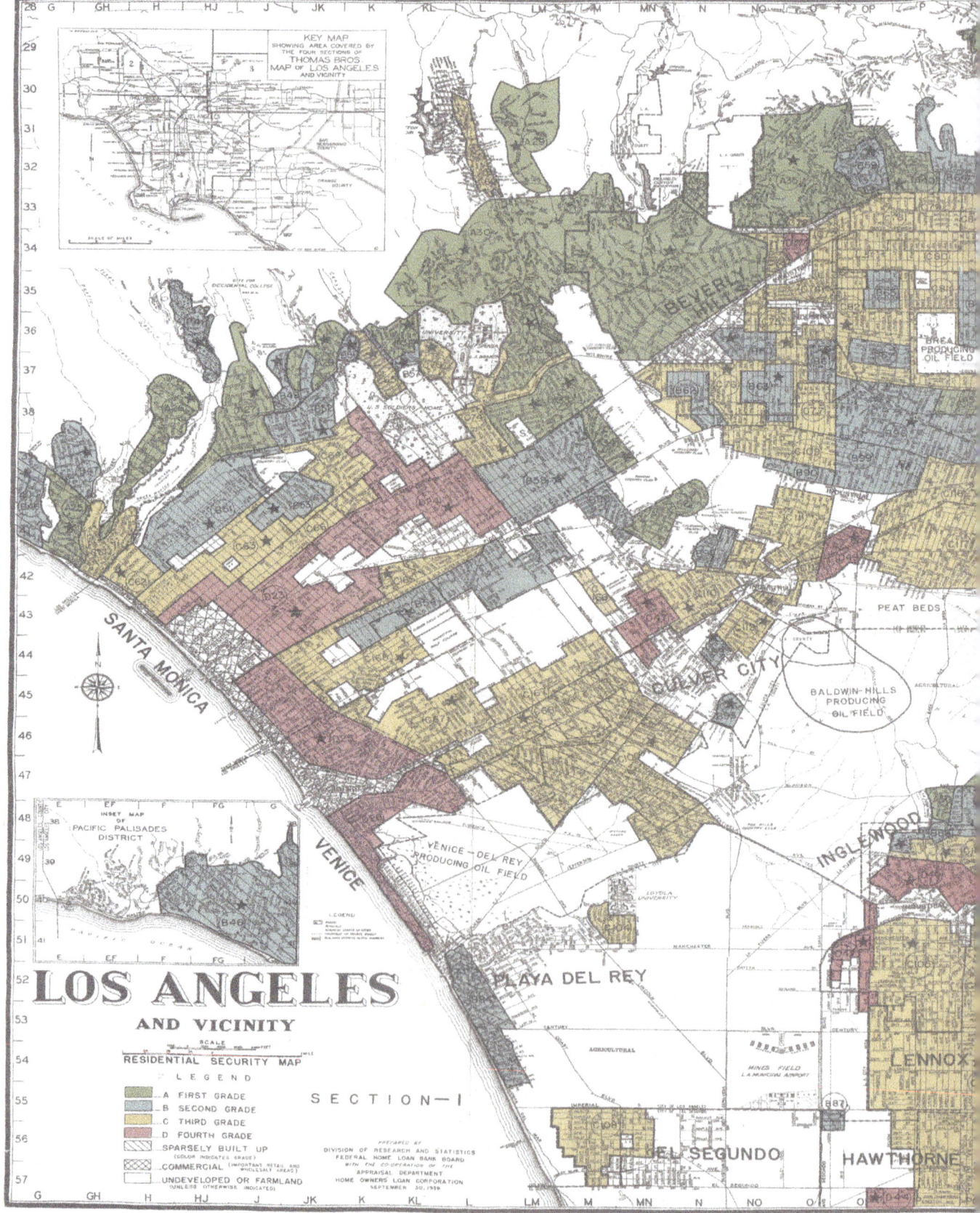

LOS ANGELES

AND VICINITY

RESIDENTIAL SECURITY MAP

L E G E N D

- A FIRST GRADE
- B SECOND GRADE
- C THIRD GRADE
- D FOURTH GRADE
- SPARSELY BUILT UP (COLOR INDICATES GRADE)
- COMMERCIAL (IMPORTANT RETAIL AND WHOLESALE AREAS)
- UNDEVELOPED OR FARMLAND (UNLESS OTHERWISE INDICATED)

S E C T I O N – 1

PREPARED BY
DIVISION OF RESEARCH AND STATISTICS
FEDERAL HOME LOAN BANK BOARD
WITH THE CO-OPERATION OF THE
APPRAISAL DEPARTMENT
HOME OWNERS LOAN CORPORATION
SEPTEMBER 20, 1939

KEY MAP
SHOWING AREA COVERED BY
THE FOUR SECTIONS OF
THOMAS BROS.
MAP OF LOS ANGELES
AND VICINITY

INSET MAP
OF
PACIFIC PALISADES
DISTRICT

SANTA MONICA

VENICE

PLAYA DEL REY

BEVERLY HILLS

CULVER CITY

BALDWIN HILLS
PRODUCING
OIL FIELD

VENICE-DEL REY
PRODUCING OIL FIELD

INGLEWOOD

PEAT BEDS

EL SEGUNDO

HAWTHORNE

LENNOX

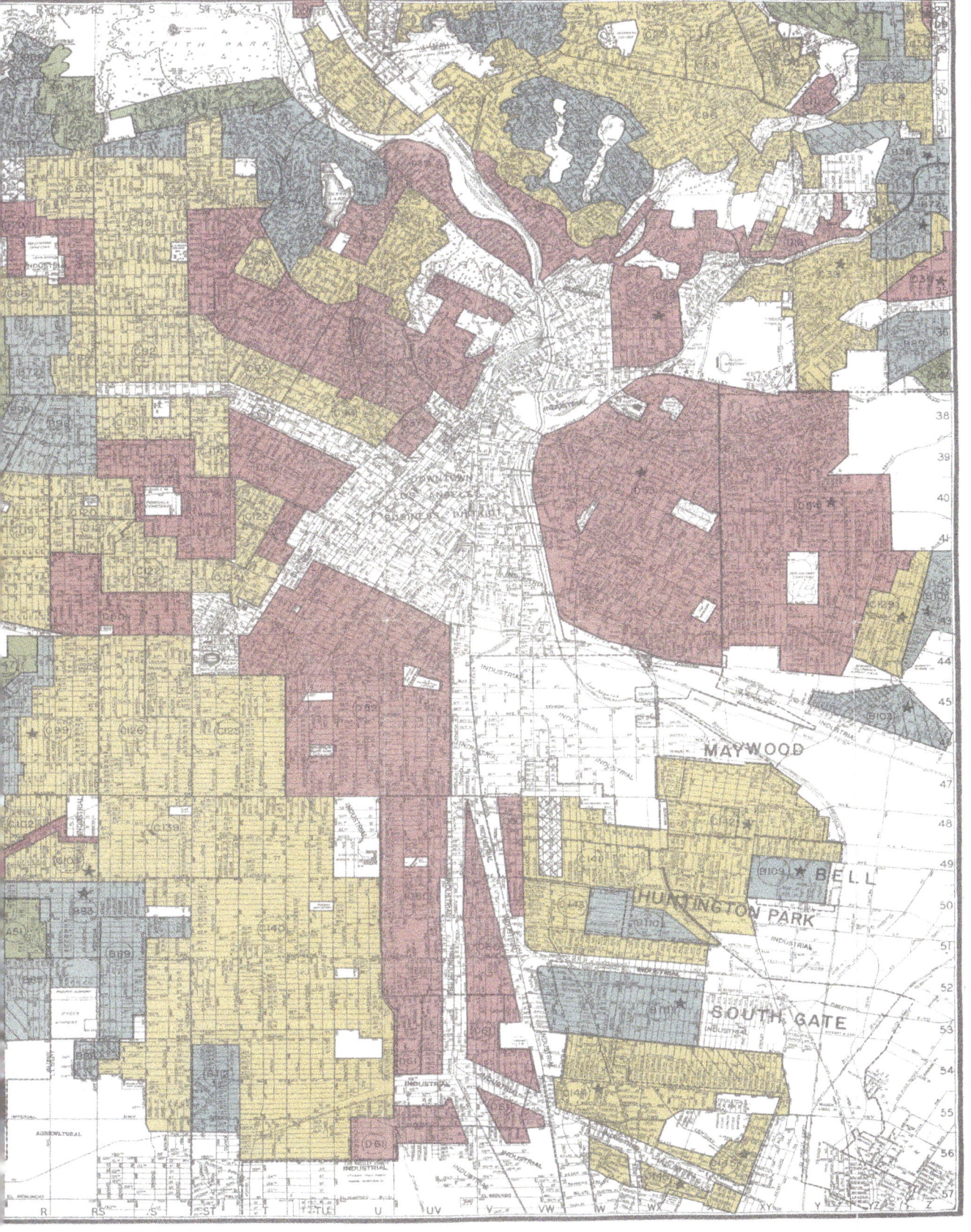

This publication was produced by DSTL Arts.

DSTL Arts is a nonprofit arts mentorship organization that inspires, teaches, and hires emerging artists from underserved communities.

To learn more about DSTL Arts, visit online at:

DSTLArts.org
@DSTLArts